Tadao Ando

Row House in Sumiyoshi
Koshino House
Kidosaki House

Residential Masterpieces 31
Tadao Ando
Row House in Sumiyoshi
Koshino House
Kidosaki House

Text by Vittorio Magnago Lampugnani
Photographed by Yukio Futagawa
Edited by Yoshio Futagawa
Art direction: Gan Hosoya

Printed and bound in Japan

ISBN 978-4-87140-564-5 C1352

Tadao Ando

Row House in Sumiyoshi

Osaka, Osaka, 1975-76

Koshino House

Ashiya, Hyogo, 1979-81/1983-84/2004-06

Kidosaki House

Setagaya, Tokyo, 1982-86

Text by Vittorio Magnago Lampugnani

Photographed by Yukio Futagawa

世界現代住宅全集31

安藤忠雄
住吉の長屋
大阪府大阪市　1975-76
小篠邸
兵庫県芦屋市　1979-81／1983-84／2004-06
城戸崎邸
東京都世田谷区　1982-86

文：ヴィットリオ・マニャーゴ・ランプニャーニ

撮影：二川幸夫　編集：二川由夫

安藤忠雄の三つの住宅──ヴィットリオ・マニャーゴ・ランプニャーニ
Three Houses by Tadao Ando *by Vittorio Magnago Lampugnani*

日本から受ける第一印象は，カオス（混沌）である。だが，注意してほしい。それは，少しも苛立たせたり不快感を与えることのないカオスである。活力があり，攻撃的で，確実な何かを秘め，強い，圧倒的なカオスなのである。さまざまな通り，不可解ともいえる電線，電柱の列，ほとんどが極端に新しくて人目を引く建築物，東京はこれらが生み出す無限大の迷路である。一方，大阪も，その整然としたグリッド状の都市構造の内部に，世界の最近の建築をすべて包含するかに見える，溢れんばかりの「虚構の美術館」を，もはや納め切れていない。歴史都市としてすばらしい京都を含めて，その他の日本の都市もまた，大部分が，過剰からまさに溢れ出さんかという印象を与える。風景は，しばしば信じ難い，どう考えても脈絡を欠いた構造物でかき乱されている。

外国人の観察に，無知は付き物である。しかし，まさにそのために，彼らが本質を見ていることも珍しくない。おそらく，世界のどこにも，日本文化ほどに危機に直面した文化はないであろう。偉大な伝統がある一方で際限のない新奇さへの願望，あるいは東洋の崇高な世界に留まりたいという願望の一方で西洋に向かう抑え難い内的要求，これらの両極の間での分裂が，あわただしく，それ故にしばしば，ただ表面的な借用を繰り返させる。建築は，その表現をより具体化し，説教じみたものにするばかりで，このような危機を映し出し際立てる以上のことをしない。

1914年に，カール・クラウスは「知識を生み出す出来事と出来事を軽く見るような知識の間に生ずる恐るべき不協和音を投影する，これらの騒々しい時代において……そのような時代には，誰も私に対して，何か留意に値する発言を期待すべきではなく……また，私は何か新しいことを言うこともできないだろう。という

のも，私が書いているところでは，騒音があまりに大きくて，それが動物か，子供たちか，それとも砲兵隊の騒音なのかを語ることすら，いまや不可能なほどなのだから。……出来事が自ずから語り，それについて何も言うべきものがない者は，ひたすらおしゃべりをする。あるいは，語るべき内容のない者は，未来に目をやり，ただ静かに佇む」と言った。80年代と90年代の日本は，あの第一次世界大戦直前のヨーロッパと共通する幾つかの特徴を示している。とくに，その文化を覆う，聴覚を麻痺させるような喧噪の存在。この騒々しさの真只中で，70年代の半ばから，一人の建築家が，未来を見つめ，ただ静かに佇んでいる。安藤忠雄である。

〈静寂の建築：一つのアプローチ〉
安藤の建築は，まさに静寂（沈黙）の建築である。飾らず，ごく限定された要素に還元され，ほとんど無に近く，その建築は，新しいものが次々に出てくる日本の都市を通り抜ける時，色彩と形態が氾濫する騒々しさの中で，見つけ出すのが困難なほどだ。しかし，その存在には重みがある。むしろ，生き残ってきた小さな歴史的モニュメントのように，安藤の建築は，東京，大阪，京都，兵庫の巨大な都市エリアの，茫然とさせる迷宮のような環境の中で，繊細だが容易に認識でき，明らかに快適な構造体を形づくっている。

安藤が静寂を生み出すのは，強迫的に厳格な形態操作，基本的な幾何学，そしてごく限定された材料の作品への利用を通してのみではない。そもそも，彼の示す単純さは，それ自体が目標ではない。それは，問題の真の解決，そして原理へと移し変えることにより無秩序状態を克服した結果生じたものなのである。

The first impression given by Japan is one of chaos. But, mark you, a chaos which is far from vexatious or unpleasant. A chaos which is vigorous, aggressive, cocksure, strong and powerful. Tokyo is an endless maze of unlikely streets, unfathomable tangles of electrical wiring and stunning buildings, almost all of which are extremely new. Within its measured rectangular grid Osaka can barely contain an overflowing *musée imaginaire* which seems to include all the world's recent architecture. Large parts of other Japanese cities, including venerable Kyoto, also give the impression of being on the point of spilling over. The landscape is littered with objects which are often unbelievable, and in any event out of context.

Foreigners view with ignorance, but, not infrequently, just because of this they can see the essentials. Perhaps there is no culture anywhere in the world which is in greater crisis than that of Japan. Torn between a great tradition and an unending desire for novelty, between a desire to remain in the sublime world of the east and a powerful thrust towards the west, it adopts in haste, and therefore only superficially. Architecture merely reflects and highlights this crisis, making its expression more concrete and didactic.

In 1914 Karl Kraus wrote, "in these clamorous times which reverberate to the dreadful cacophony of events which bring forth knowledge and knowledge which spurns events. At such a time no one should expect me to say anything of any note;...nor could I say anything new, because where I write the noise is so loud that it is now impossible to tell whether it is the noise of animals, children or just artillery... Those who now have nothing to say, because events

speak for themselves, persist in chattering. Those who do have anything to say look to the future and stay silent." Japan in the 80s and 90s has more than one feature in common with Europe on the eve of the First World War. If nothing else, the deafening clamor in its culture. Amidst this noise, since the middle 70s one architect has looked to the future and remained silent: Tadao Ando.

The Architecture of Silence: One Approach
Ando's architecture is truly the architecture of silence. Bare, reduced to very few essentials and apparently made of almost nothing, it is not easily discovered amid the hubbub of boisterous multi-colored shapes when passing through burgeoning Japanese cities. But its presence has weight. Rather like small surviving historical monuments, Ando's buildings form a fine but easily recognized and undoubtedly comforting fabric in the stupefying labyrinths of the immense urban areas of Tokyo, Osaka, Kyoto and Hyogo.

It is not only through obsessively strict formalism, elementary geometry and the use of very few materials that Ando achieves silence. His simplicity is not a front. It is the product of the true solution of a problem, the conquest of a state of disorder which is transformed into discipline. In fact on his own terms and in those well-defined cases where he himself has made a specific statement, Ando resolves the contradictions between the two cultures, of the east and of the west, translating both to a very high level of abstraction. Thus the pure spaces of Euclidean geometry are combined with those equally pure spaces which nevertheless incorporate the

実際，その意図通りに，そして彼特有の表現にまで十分に推敲し得た場合には，安藤は，ともに一つの高度な抽象レベルに引き上げることによって，東洋と西洋の二つの文化の矛盾対立を解いている。たとえば，ユークリッド幾何学の純粋空間が，微妙に非対称な力を内包する日本古来の建築の純粋空間と統合される。ギリシャ神殿のみならず日本の神社仏閣にも見られた，構造と空間境界の，つまり建物の骨格と皮膚の同一化が，（断熱面での多くの問題を抱え込みながら）実に注意深く施工された打放しコンクリートによって，ここに再現されている。彼の打放しコンクリートは，ル・コルビュジエの「ベトン・ブリュ（生のコンクリート）」とは異なり，それ自体の容積ではなく，それが内部に包み込み限定する空間の方を強調するものである。あるいはまた，すでにフランク・ロイド・ライトとかミース・ファン・デル・ローエらが日本から「輸入」し近代運動の不可欠な要素としていた，あの流動的な空間も，新奇さとか過去との断絶ではなく，一人の日本人建築家の筆が描き出す伝統との連続性として再現されている。たぶん安藤作品の傑出した特徴であろう，劇的な熱情には陥ることなく巧みに編成された光のシンフォニーもまた，ローマのパンテオンと京都の竜安寺（石庭）に共通するものであった。そして最後に，すべての近代西洋と絶妙にして典型化された日本的伝統の，両者の象徴ともいえる単純さが，安藤の試みを，欧米の長い建築文化が生んだ最良のものに結び付けているのである。

　安藤が実際，ル・コルビュジエ，ルイス・カーン，アルド・ロッシ，そしてカール・アンドレとかリチャード・セラらの実験的試みを，最大限の注意を払って追ってきたことに疑いはない。しかし，彼は遠く離れ，有利な日本の地から彼らを観察してきたのであり，他のほとんどの日本人建築家とは異なって，その地点にしっか

りと根を下ろしたままである。結果として彼は，軽率な文化的借用，質の悪いコラージュ，さらに悪い奴隷的な模倣行為などの誘惑に決して負けることがなかった。彼は幾分のプライドをもって，日本的な建築家であり続けているのである。

　以上のような一般的なコメントは，安藤忠雄の建築作品に初めてアプローチする際には有用かもしれない。ただし，ただ見かけ上だけアプローチし易そうに見える作品にはふさわしい，ゆっくりとした，用心深い，ほとんど躊躇しながらのアプローチである。より深く知るには，われわれは，一般的なものから特殊なものへと進む必要がある。言い換えれば，われわれは，安藤の建築全体を批判的に分析するところから，彼特有の建築創造を分析する方向に進まねばならないであろう。

　ここでは，この目的のために，3作品を選んだ。大阪の住吉区にある「住吉の長屋」（「東邸」），兵庫県の芦屋近郊の「小篠邸」，そして東京の世田谷区にある「城戸崎邸」である。これらの3住宅は，彼の作歴において，時間的な隔たりを有している。1975年から76年にかけて設計され建設された「住吉の長屋」は，最初の，ゆえに安藤の最も初期の代表作と見なしうる。1979年から81年にかけて成立した「小篠邸」は，1983〜84年に増築されているが，「住吉の長屋」よりは若干新しい。1982年から85年にかけて設計され，1986年に竣工した「城戸崎邸」は，厳密にはそう新しいとは言い難い。しかしながら，今日的であるという質は，安藤の建築に適用される理念としては最もふさわしくないものの一つであって，彼の建築は，全体として判然とこの質から隔てられていることを，念頭に置いている。この3作品が，住宅という課題に対する安藤の建築的探求における幾度かの転換をそれぞれに象徴するものとして描き得る理由は，他にもあ

asymmetrical stresses of ancient Japanese architecture. The identity between a structure and the boundaries of space, between the bones and the skin of a building, which is present in Greek temples as it is in Buddhist temples and Shinto shrines, is offered again (despite the enormous problems of heat insulation) by the very carefully worked exposed concrete which, unlike Le Corbusier's *béton brut*, emphasizes not its own bulk but the empty space which it bounds and defines. Fluid space, which Frank Lloyd Wright and Ludwig Mies van der Rohe had already "imported" from Japan and made an integral part of the Modern Movement, reappears not as a novelty and a break with the past, but, drawn with the brush of a Japanese architect, as continuity. A symphony of light ably orchestrated without succumbing to theatrical temptations, perhaps the most prominent feature of Ando's work, is common to both the Pantheon in Rome and the Ryoanji temple. Finally, simplicity, the emblem of all the modern West and the most exquisitely and exclusively Japanese tradition, links Ando's probing with the best examples of European and American architectural culture.

There can be no doubt that Ando has in fact followed the experiments of Le Corbusier, Louis Kahn, Aldo Rossi, and even those of Carl Andre and Richard Serra, with great attention. But he has observed these from his remote Japanese vantage point, to which, unlike most of his compatriot architects, he has remained firmly bound. As a consequence he has never yielded to the temptation of facile cultural borrowing, ill-considered collage or, even worse, slavish copying. He has remained, and not without some pride, a Japanese architect.

These comments of a general nature may be of use when approaching the architectural work of Tadao Ando for the first time a slow, cautious, almost hesitant approach, appropriate to such work, which only appears to be easy of approach. For a deeper knowledge we will have to pass from the general to the specific. We will, in other words, have to pass from a critical analysis of Ando's architecture as a whole, to an analysis of his specific architectural creations.

We have chosen three for this purpose: *the Row House in Sumiyoshi* (*Azuma House*) in the Sumiyoshi ward of Osaka, *the Koshino House* near Ashiya in Hyogo prefecture, and *the Kidosaki House* in the Setagaya ward of Tokyo. These three houses are not recent in chronological terms. Thus *the Row House in Sumiyoshi*, which was designed and built during 1975-76, can be regarded as being the first and therefore the oldest major work carried out by Ando. *The Koshino House*, which dates from 1979-81, with an extension in 1983-84, is only slightly more recent. And even *the Kidosaki House*, which was designed during 1982-85, and completed in 1986, cannot strictly be said to be new. However the quality of being up-to-date is one of the least appropriate ideas to be applied to Ando's architecture, which is wholly and manifestly dissociated from this. There are other reasons why the three houses can be described as symbolic junctures in Ando's architectural exploration of residential design—the differences in their plans (the first is extremely small and elemental; the second exceptionally large, but also elemental;

る。たとえば，その平面構成の違い（第1作品は極端に小さく要素的で，第2作品は例外的に大きいが同じく要素的であり，第3作品は大きくかつ複合的である），そのコンテクストの違い（第1作品は極度に高密な下町にあり，第2作品は山の中の樹木と草地に恵まれた敷地に置かれ，第3作品は中間的な密度の住宅地区にある），そして建築形態がこれらの与条件に対応し，それを固有の質にまで高めていく際の，それぞれに特有のラディカルなアプローチが示す違いである。

〈住吉の長屋（東邸）〉
「住吉の長屋」は，大阪の中心部，住吉区にある。木造でありながら第二次世界大戦をも生きのびた小規模な住宅群の並びに建つ，ごく小さな並び家（長屋）である。そこにあった伝統的な小住宅から建築類型は受け継がずに，外と接触するエリアと敷地境界のみを継承して，建替えが行われている。

　通り側からは，ほとんど，それと気づかない。あるいは，良くとも，そのファサードの見る者を苛立たせるほどの単純さの故に，存在に気づくのである。この住宅は公道には信じ難い矩形の鉄筋コンクリートの壁で面し，しかもその壁には狭い，再び矩形の玄関口が切り抜かれている。この玄関は，道路から一段のステップを上がれば，すぐそこにある。他には何もない。窓も，バルコニーも，コーニスも，基礎階もない。玄関扉も見えない。ファサードの壁の縦長の切抜きは空虚なままに，内部に極小の玄関ホールを抱き込んでいる。この極小のホールに，上からトップライトの光が落ちてくる。そして，ここから住宅内部へと玄関扉が開くのである。しかし，先に急ぐのはやめて，しばし通りに佇み，そのファサードを観察しようではないか。すでに述べたように，ファサードには建築

的要素は何もないかに見える。しかし，ファサードの無の表現は巧みに演出されたものであって，注意深い目には次第に見えてくる多くの建築的特徴が内包されている。たとえば，打放しコンクリートの裸の壁体はすばらしい技術で施工され，その表面に残された型枠の跡は，それだけ控え目な幾何学的なデザインとなるが，この幾何学が，潜んでいる繊細な構成原理を解く鍵を与えてくれる。ファサードの長方形は，二つのほぼ正方形が上下に積み重ねられたものと見なすことができるが，さらに，各々の正方形は細い水平線によって上下方向に3層に分けられ，それはあたかも紙か木のパネルか外装の石貼りの層のようである。何本かの水平線のなかでも，二つの「正方形」が接するところでは，その水平線がさらにくっきりと浮かび上がり，これがこの建物の1階と2階を分ける線である。また，上の「正方形」は半層分だけ高くなっているが，この場合，水平線がコーニス（軒蛇腹）の役割を果たしている。左右対称の中心軸は2本の垂直線によって強調され，その垂直線は「コーニス」の中心から矩形の玄関口の真ん中まで走っている。それは，むしろ高さを誇張されたキーストーンのようでもある。ファサードに見られる唯一の建築的要素である玄関口は，優美なプロポーションを有するが，コンクリートの壁体にすぱっと切り抜かれているに過ぎない。

　このように隠された形で複雑に分節されてはいるものの，この住宅の正面ファサードからは，内部の構成については何も，ほとんど何も窺うことができない。それを知るためには，われわれは，敷地を跨がねばならない。これは，すぱっと切られたエッジをもつ玄関口とその象徴性を帯びた堅牢なステップに導かれる行為である。そして，玄昌石のスレートに覆われた一種のミニチュア化された基壇が，建物前面の幅一杯に広がり，この住宅の1階の床全面を覆う材料を予

the third large and complex), the differences in their contexts (the first is located in an extremely densely inhabited central urban area; the second is set down in mountain parkland; the third is in a medium density residential area), and the identical radical approach through which the constructed shape reacts to these conditions and transforms them into its intrinsic qualities.

Row House in Sumiyoshi (Azuma House)
The Row House in Sumiyoshi rises in the very center of Osaka, in the Sumiyoshi ward. It is a very small row house in a row of other equally small houses which despite being built of wood survived the Second World War. It in fact replaces one of these small traditional residential buildings, adopting its surface area and boundaries, but not its type.

From the street it is almost unnoticed. Or, better, it is noticed only because of the almost irritating simplicity of its facade. The house fronts the public roadway with an incredible rectangular wall of reinforced concrete which is pierced only by a narrow, again rectangular, entrance slot, which is gained by climbing a single step. Nothing more. No window, no balcony, no cornice, no base. Not even a door. The slot is left bare and invites entrance into a minuscule hall which even a skylight barely draws from darkness. It is only from this that the entrance door finally opens. But we must not get ahead of ourselves. Let's for the moment remain on the street and observe the facade. This, as we have noted, is made of virtually nothing. But this almost nothing is skillfully orchestrated and

includes a number of architectural features which only gradually reveal themselves to the attentive eye. The bare wall of exposed reinforced concrete is constructed with great mastery, and the marks left on the surface by the formwork trace an unobtrusive geometrical design which provides a key to the subtle rules of its composition. The slender rectangle of the facade is seen to be two almost square elements placed vertically one above the other, each consisting of three layers of concrete picked out by fine horizontal lines, as if they were rows of paper and wood panels or courses of facing stone. A more pronounced line at the point where the two "squares" join acts as a story marker, the other, at the top of the second "square," distinguishes a half layer of cement added by way of a cornice. The central axis of symmetry is marked by a double vertical line which starting from the center of the "cornice" runs to the middle of the entrance slot, rather like a keystone of exaggerated height. The entrance slot, the only true architectural feature in the facade, is elegantly proportioned and roughly cut into the concrete wall.

The front of the house, although complexly subdivided in this way, reveals nothing or almost nothing of its internal organization. To discover this we must cross the threshold——an action which is invited not only by the entrance slot with its bare edges and its symbolic solitary step——a sort of miniature slate platform which occupies the full width of the frontage and provides an introduction to the material which paves the ground floor of the house.

Passing through the extremely small hall, or vestibule, we gain

め示している。

その極端に小さなホール，つまりヴェスティビュールであり玄関室でもある空間を通って，われわれは居間の側部に入る。この居間に踏み込むやいなや，中庭に向かって開くフランス窓が正面に見える。台所と食堂が居間の反対側にあって，同じ中庭に開いている。つまり，台所と食堂は，中庭によって居間と隔てられているのだが，なお同じ階にある。台所と食堂の空間を通って，浴室にアクセスする。

この中庭から，それを囲む一方の壁に沿って設けられた階段によって2階へと進む。2階には二つの寝室がある。それは，玄関ホールの上に付いていたのと同じようなトップライトをともなう主寝室と，子供室になっている。1階で居間と台所，食堂が向かいあっていたのと同じ形で，両寝室も同じ2階で向きあっている。両者はともに大きなガラス窓で中庭に開き，中庭の中央に奥行方向にかかるコンクリート・ブリッジによって結ばれている（と同時に，分離されている）。清らかな青みがかった灰色の表面と，その型枠による幾何学的な痕跡の簡素な表情などをともなう鉄筋コンクリートが，すべての内部空間の性質を決定し，付加的な表現はどのようなものであれ，そこから厳しく排除されている。コンクリートと組み合わされるのは，ドアと窓の大きなガラス面，そのスティール枠，1階の玄昌石と2階の木のフローリングなどである。

この住宅の3分割された平面は，この上なく厳格な幾何学に従っている。その三つの主要要素は一致し，基本平面の執拗なまでの正確さにおけるほとんど知覚できないほどの変形の試みのみが，生活するには避けられない与条件との不承不承の妥協を示している。しかしながら，このことは，決して好ましいこと

ではない。個々の空間へのアクセスは，実際のところ，中庭を介して行われるのだが，この中庭は外部空間であって天候から保護されていない。だから，寒気，雨，雪に見舞われようとも，人は必ず一度は外に出なければならない。唯一の例外も，この原則的な不便さを確認させるものでしかない。直に屋内でアクセスできるのが浴室のみなのだが，それも台所，食堂を通らねばならない。西洋的基準（そして今や，国際的基準）で考えれば，「住吉の長屋」は，必ずしも使い易くないし，住み易くもない，優しさに欠ける住宅ということになろうか。

これは無論，早まった，皮相な判断でしかない。それでは，この小住宅に明らかな，議論を呼び起こそうという目的の存在が見落される。目的が本質的にこの生活の問題に焦点を合わせるものだということも，考慮されていない。

少なくともそれなりに徹底して検討すれば，安藤忠雄に関する限り，この「住吉の長屋」も，ル・コルビュジエの「ドミノ・ハウス」，ルートヴィヒ・ミース・ファン・デル・ローエの「煉瓦造田園住宅」，そしてモスクワに建てられたコンスタンチン・メルニコフの自邸などと同様に，（広義の）モデル住宅なのである。それは，哲学的原理を具体化し，表現を与え，この建築家の仕事に本質的なテーマをデザインするものである（そして実際，「住吉の長屋」が喚起した問題は，安藤の作品に繰り返し現れている）。しかも，極端に，根源的に，そして恐らく誇張して，しかし効果的な方法で，それを行っている。

足を踏み入れたとき直ちに感じ取れるこの作品の第一のテーマは，陰翳，より良くいえば自然光を調節しつつ巧みに利用することである。1933年に作家の谷崎潤一郎が『陰翳礼讃』を書いているが，それは，かつては東洋文化にとって極めて大切なものであった，光のやわらかなグラデーションの伝統的な利用への

access to the side of the living room, where we face a French window opening onto an inner courtyard. On the same level, across and thus separate from the living room, a kitchen/dining room also opens onto the courtyard.

From the inner courtyard a stairway to one side gives access to the upper level. Here two bedrooms, one for adults (with a skylight similar to that which gives light to the entrance) and one for children, face each other as the kitchen and living room do on the ground floor. Both open onto the courtyard with wide windows and are connected (and separated at the same time) by a central concrete bridge which spans the full length of the courtyard. The reinforced concrete, with its smooth gray-blue surface and austere texture with traces from the formwork, determines the nature of all the internal spaces, from which all forms of rendering are strictly banished. The concrete is flanked by the glass of the large doors and windows, the steel of the frames, the slate of the ground-floor paving and the wood of the upper floor.

The tripartite plan has an absolutely strict geometry. The three main elements are identical, and only almost imperceptible variations in the implacable precision of the basic plan mark a reluctant compromise with the imperatives of life. This however is somewhat unpleasant. Access to the individual spaces is in fact provided via an inner courtyard, which is not in any way protected from weather, and one is therefore always obliged to go outside, regardless of cold, rain, or snow. The only exception merely confirms the rule of inconvenience; the bathroom is only accessible from the kitchen/dining

room. Measured by Western (now international) standards of comfort *the Row House in Sumiyoshi* is inhospitable, not very practical, and thus not very easy to live in.

This is of course a hasty and superficial verdict. It takes no account of the eminently contentious purpose of the little building. Neither does it consider that its purpose essentially concentrates on precisely this question of living.

There is no doubt, at least on reasonably thorough investigation, that *the Row House in Sumiyoshi* is, as far as Tadao Ando is concerned, a show house, like *the Maison Dom-Ino* for Le Corbusier, like *the Brick Country House* for Ludwig Mies van der Rohe, like the house which Konstantin Melnikov built for himself in Moscow. It embodies and gives expression to the philosophical principles and design themes fundamental to the work of its architect (and in fact the questions raised by *the Row House in Sumiyoshi* resurge periodically in Ando's work). It does so in a manner which is extreme, radical, and perhaps exaggerated, but effective.

The first theme, which can be felt as soon as one sets foot in the house, is that of shadow, or better, the modulation of natural light. In 1933, writer Junichiro Tanizaki published the book *In Praise of Shadows*, as a sort of poetic manual which encouraged a return to the traditional use of soft gradations of light, which was once very dear to eastern culture. Ando has treasured the lucid admonishments of this renowned poet. At the most symbolic points in the house (the entrance, the bedroom), he has provided skylights which hark back to the old *tsukiage-mado* and emphasize the change in

回帰を勧める，詩的な入門書のようなものであった。安藤は，同時代の詩人から発せられる明晰そのものの忠告を大切にしているが，この住宅の最も象徴的な場所（玄関と寝室）には昔の突き上げ窓を思わせるトップライト（天窓）を付け，居間にも，調整する媒介空間を経由して導き入れることで，昼から夜への光の変化を強調している。居間を含めて諸室は，通り側にも建物の裏側にも開かず，中庭に向かってのみ開いている。その中庭で，自然光は周囲の壁（による複雑な反射など）によって和らげられ，内部化されたものになっているのである。

しかし，この中庭は，太陽とか月の光に対してフィルターの役割を果たすよりも，もっと影響力の大きい重要な働きをする。つまり，高度に人工的な方法で，住宅の壁の中にいくつかの自然を切り取るという仕事である。これが，安藤忠雄の建築が目指す2番目の大きなテーマになる。彼にとっては建築は，それを通して自然を見，感じるための一つの手段に他ならない。しかし自然は，あるがままでは建築に組み込むことはできない（そしてこのことは，どのようなタイプであれ屋内に自然のままに存在する緑に対して日本人建築家が抱く深い嫌悪感を説明する）。それには，適切な調整が必要である。中庭は，この調整を効果的なものにする最善の手法の一つである。中庭においては毎日，自然が異なる姿を投げかける。中庭は，この住宅で繰り広げられる生活の核であり，都市で失われつつある光，風，雨といった自然の感覚（現象）を住居に引き込む装置である。

「住吉の長屋」に見られるように，機能性，居住性を犠牲にしてまで，居室相互の連絡を断ち切ってしまうような，いわば異質なものを外から人工的に挿入することが，安藤にとってそれほど重要なのであろうか。おそらく，そうなのである。しかし問題は発生せず，ここで一般化して誤った説明をする必要はない。

というのも，安藤の建築的探求の3番目のテーマが，まさに生活そのものに向けられ，住宅における機能的な快適性というコンセプト（そして，それが果たして必要か，また望むべきものか）を個別な事例で問い直すところにあるからである。

「私は，厳しい生活の中からどういう新しい生活（パターン）を引き出して発展させることができるかを問うていきたいと思っている。そして，生活に格調のようなものを与えるために，秩序が必要だと感じている。秩序の中で生活していくことは，人間をかなり規制することになるが，それによって，一般的ではないものがその人の中に育まれていくのではないかと考えている。機能的な基礎を十分に確かめた上で，今度は，機能から建築を遠ざけることを考えたい。言いかえれば，建築はどれだけ機能を追求できるかを確かめたいし，それを追求した後は，どれだけ機能から建築を遠ざけることができるかを確かめたい。この遠ざける距離に，建築の意味がかかっているのではないか」。これは彼の信条であるが，「住吉の長屋」を設計してから5年後の1980年に，それまでの自らの体験を総括する形で，彼が書いたものである。キーセンテンスは，この冒頭にある：「厳しい生活の中からどういう新しい生活（パターン）を引き出して発展させることができるかを問うていきたいと思っている」。この日本人建築家は，自らの文化

light from day to night by letting it in, in filtered form, to the living space. The rooms too do not open onto the street or onto the rear of the house, but onto an inner courtyard, where natural light is already softened and domesticated by the walled perimeter.

The inner courtyard however has a much greater and more important task than that of acting as a first filter for the light of the sun or the moon. It is that of bringing a fragment of nature within the walls of the house, in a highly artificial way. This is the second great theme in Tadao Ando's architecture. For him architecture is a means through which nature can be seen and felt. But nature cannot be incorporated into architecture as it is (and this explains the Japanese architect's profound aversion for any type of domestic greenery); it must be appropriately mediated. A courtyard is one of the best ways of effecting this mediation. In the courtyard, nature presents a different aspect of itself each day. The courtyard is the nucleus of life that unfolds within the house and is a device to introduce natural phenomena such as light, wind, and rain that are being forgotten in the city.

Is this task of subordinating functionality and habitability, as in *the Row House in Sumiyoshi*, to a kind of artificial obstacle in the flow of spatial connections between one room and another so important to Ando? Probably so. The problem does not arise however, and misrepresentation is not necessary. Because the third great theme of Ando's architectural exploration is living itself, more specifically questioning the concept (and the necessity and desirability) of functional comfort in a house.

"I am interested in discovering what new life patterns can be extracted and developed from living under severe conditions. Furthermore, I felt that order is necessary to give life dignity. Establishing order imposes restrictions, but I believe it cultivates extraordinary things in people. I believe in removing architecture from function after ensuring the observation of functional basis. In other words, I like to see how far architecture can pursue function and then, after the pursuit has been made, to see how far architecture can be removed from function. The significance of architecture is found in the distance between it and function." This was his creed, and Ando wrote it down in 1980, five years after he had drawn the plans for *the Row House in Sumiyoshi*, to some extent summarizing his experience there. The key sentence is still the first: "I am interested in discovering what new life patterns can be extracted and developed from living under severe conditions." Ando sets an asceticism derived from his own cultural tradition, which is not thereby obscured by any nationalism, against the rampant consumerism clearly derived from the west. In an increasingly uniform world where anything can be had at any time, for payment of course, although only as a surrogate, Ando offers the extreme luxury of a new self-imposed discipline which enforces reflection about real values and the experience of many realities: heat, cold sun, rain,

的伝統から引き出した，しかしいかなるナショナリズムにも曇らされていない禁欲主義を，明らかに西洋からもたらされた圧倒的な消費文化に対抗させている。いかなる場合にも代金さえ払えば，ただ代用品に過ぎないものも含めて，とにかく何でも手に入る画一化の激しい世界において，安藤は，真の価値について深く考え（代用品ではない）リアリティを実際に体験することを求める，極端に贅沢ともいえる原則を，新たに自らに課してみせている。つまり，暑さ,寒さ,太陽,雨,風,雪,光,闇などの多様なリアリティとか，中間状態でその多様なリアリティが生み出す無限のグラデーションとニュアンスを，実際に体験することである。極限まで簡素さを求める条件設定（われわれ西洋人は，その例をフランシスコ派修道士に求めることができるかもしれない）が，最高の洗練と崇高な豊かさをもたらしている。

〈小篠邸〉
ここに述べてきたことはすべて，57平方メートルの敷地面積に，65平方メートルの延床面積という現に簡素で「貧しい」建築に関しては，もっともと思われよう。しかしながら，これからもう少し詳しく見るが，安藤のもう一つの作品である「小篠邸」に関しては，議論は別の形でありそうである。これはもはや都市住宅ではなくて山の中の住宅であって，日本の都市内の狭く高密なコンテクストと比較する時，その規模が決定的にそして例外的に贅沢な別荘と見る必要がある。1,000平方メートル強の敷地面積に，285平方メートルほどの延床面積を有している。そのように恵まれた状況でもなお，禁欲主義について語ることができようか。この問いに答える前に，建築本体がいかなるものか，まず，それを描写してみよう。

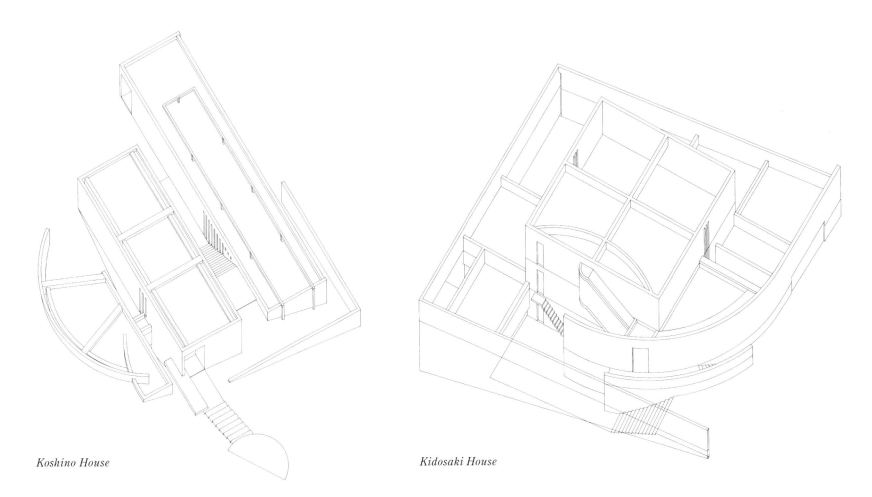

Koshino House

Kidosaki House

wind, snow, light, dark, and the infinite gradations and nuances which life creates between such extremes. Conditions of strict simplicity (which we westerners might refer to as being Franciscan) bring forth maximum refinement, and the most sublime richness.

Koshino House

All this might appear plausible for a simple and "poor" building as *the Row House in Sumiyoshi* undoubtedly is, with only 65 square meters of useful area obtained from a plot only 57 square meters. The argument would appear however to be different for *the Koshino House*, another architectural work by Ando which we will now set about observing more closely. This is no longer an urban residence, but a house in the mountains, a second home whose size, especially in the cramped context of Japan, must be regarded as being deci-

sively and exceptionally luxurious—some 285 square meters of useful space in a small park of 1,000 square meters. Is it still possible to speak of asceticism when faced with such opulence? Before attempting to answer this question we will describe the architecture to which it refers. *The Koshino House* consists of three separate units, arranged parallel to each other and rotated through approximately 45 degrees with respect to the boundaries of the site to obtain better exposure to the sun and preserve the ancient trees of the park. The site, located in the middle of a splendid nature reserve on mount Rokko near the city of Ashiya, is quite steep. Because of this, and so as not to spoil its profile, the three parts of the building are partly buried. Access is gained to the house from the top, a little like Mies van der Rohe's *Tugendhat House*. A short drive bounded by metal railings on the right and a concrete bench on the left leads

「小篠邸」は，互いに平行に，そしてより日照を多くし既存の古い樹木を保存するために敷地境界に対してはほぼ45度の角度に振られた，独立した三つの棟からなる。芦屋の近く六甲山のすばらしく緑豊かな国立公園内にあって，その敷地はかなり傾斜している。それ故に，またその地形の輪郭を破壊しないためにも，その3棟は，部分的に地中に埋められている。住宅へのアクセスは一番高いところにあって，ミース・ファン・デル・ローエの「トゥーゲントハット邸」に少し似ている。右手に金属の手摺，左手にコンクリートのベンチがある短い，エントランスまでの導入路は，主棟に対し非対称で，左にずれている。この直方体のコンクリート・ボックスである主棟には，上の階にエントランスの他，寝室，化粧室と書斎が入る。エントランスからまっすぐに下りる階段は，広々とした下の階に達する。この下の階では，2層分の天井高を有する広い居間にキッチンと食堂が接続する。居間は，サイズの異なる2枚の大きなスティール・サッシュの窓と，（エントランスから下りてくる階段と同じ側の）周壁にそって細長く平屋根に開けられたトップライトによって，採光される。トップライトからの自然光は，打放しコンクリートの広い壁の表面で，波のうねりのような変化を見せる。その仕上げは，極端に抑制されている。その象徴的な例が細長い食卓であって，それは食堂部分はヨーロッパ風に標準的高さを有し普通の（無論われわれ西洋人の視点での「普通」だが）使われ方をしているが，食堂の床より居間の床が2段ほど上がっているために，居間では東洋風の高さに変わり，床に膝をついて利用すると丁度よい。全体が豪華な印象を与える構図を形づくり，光と影の巧みな操作に支えられた空間とオブジェが，ピート・モンドリアンとかテオ・ファン・ドゥースブルフらのほとんど空間の詩学に近いものを知ることを通して再生する，16世紀日本の茶室建築（数寄屋）の

ような伝統建築を，さらに蒸留して得られる名状しがたい調和の精妙なルールに従っている。この主棟の南側に，同じ幅だが長く低い直方体の従棟が配される。この中には，1本の真っすぐな片側廊下に沿って八つの個室ユニット（子供室とゲスト・ルーム）が並び，西端に浴室がある。この直線廊下の側壁の中央部分には8本の縦のスリット，そして東端には大きな窓が開けられている。個室は，日本の伝統的な四畳半を基本とする広さになっている。部屋はすべて南に面し，南側の吹きさらしの列柱廊とさらに外を平行に走る自立した壁（塀）が，外部に対しスクリーンとなる。

　この主従の2棟の内部連絡は，キッチンの裏側を通る地下の廊下で行われ，この連絡通路は，従棟の廊下に直角に接続する。この2棟の間には，その短辺側が開放された長方形の，一種の中庭がある。その東には，地形の傾斜を残した，（中庭の延長とも外の庭園とも見える）若干性格の曖昧な空間が現れる。西は，この中庭の幅でそのまま大きな階段となり，従棟の平らな屋上へのアクセスを提供している。カプリの「ヴィラ・マラパルテ」のためにアダルベルト・リベラが構想し実現させた外部階段を参照したことは，明白である。リベラのあの階段と同様に，安藤の場合も，それは階段であると同時に屋根でもあり，建築的なメタファであると同時に，元々すばらしい眺めを誇っていた自然を組織しようとする大きな身振りでもある。あるいは，あの場合同様にこれもまた，私的なものであるにもかかわらず社会的モニュメントをほのめかし，現実には存在しない儀式を完結させるために，最上階に置かれた祭壇まで上がるように誘っているかのようである。さらにはあのリベラの階段がそうであったように，それは実際はどこにも到達しないのであって，最上階は何もない空間であり，雨風に晒されたテラスに過

asymmetrically to the body of the main fabric. This, a reinforced concrete rectangle, contains on its upper level, in addition to the entrance, the main bedroom, a bathroom and a small study. A straight stairway leads down to the more extensive lower level, occupied by the vast double height living room, the dining area and the kitchen. The living room is lit by two large rectangular windows with steel frames of different size as well as long narrow skylights which pierce the flat ceiling along the perimeter walls, through which surges of changing light skim across the gigantic surfaces of the bare concrete walls. The furnishings are extremely spare. One emblematic detail is the long narrow dining table which in the dining area has the standard western height and can therefore be used conventionally (from our point of view, of course), while in the living area, by comparison, it is only slightly raised, to the traditional Japanese height, and can therefore be used kneeling on the floor. The whole forms a grandiose composition where space and objects assisted by the clever play of light and shadow follow the subtle rules of an inexpressible harmony distilled from the traditional architecture of the sixteenth-century Japanese tea house (*sukiya*) revisited with the knowledge of the near plastic poetry of Piet Mondrian or Theo van Doesburg. To the south of the first part of the building there lies the second, a rectangle of the same width, but longer and lower. This contains eight small bedrooms (for children and guests) in an orderly line along a corridor, and, at the western end, a bathroom. The corridor is lit by eight tall narrow slits in its central portion and by a large window at the east-facing end. The

rooms are traditional Japanese four-and-a-half *tatami* rooms. They all open to the south, screened on the outside by a kind of portico and partly by a retaining wall which runs parallel to the building.

The two parts of the building are connected together by an underground passageway which begins behind the kitchen and runs perpendicularly into the corridor serving the bedroom wing. Between the two buildings there is a sort of inner courtyard open on its two narrower sides. To the east its slightly ambiguous space merges with the hillslope. To the west a stairway which occupies the full width of the court yard provides geometrical access to the flat parapeted roof of the second building. The reference to the outside staircase conceived and constructed by Adalberto Libera for *the Villa Malaparte* in Capri is immediate. Like that one, Ando's stairway is not only a staircase but also a roof. Like that one, it is an architectural metaphor and at the same time a grand gesture organizing a spectacular nature which is otherwise left intact. Like that one, it makes allusion to a social monument and invites one to ascend towards an altar which is only there to consummate a non-existent rite. Like that one, it in fact leads nowhere, to an empty space, to a terrace exposed to the weather, an unreal setting for adoration not of the sun, as in the legendary Mediterranean island, but of the moon.

The third part of the building is on the left of the central rectangle on entering. Laid out on an approximately semicircular plan, its circular wall contrasts with the nearby straight boundary of the site, thus formally shutting off the architectural composition from

ぎず，地中海の伝説の島で行われたという太陽崇拝ではなくて，月を崇拝するための架空の祭壇なのである。

　3番目の棟は，エントランスに進むとき，主棟の左側に見える。ほぼ半円形にレイアウトされ，その円弧を描く壁は，道路側の直線的な敷地境界と対照をなし，外の世界からこの建築全体を隔離しようとしているかのようである。この棟は増築であって，当初の計画にはなかったものであるが，一つの住宅の論理的帰結，そして有機的拡張のように見える。内部には，デザイナーであるこの家の女主人のアトリエと化粧室が含まれる。この内部化された空間はほぼ全体が地中に埋められているが，その分だけ強い表現をもったコンクリート壁によって守られている。東側では，砂丘から考古学的遺構が顔を出すように，建築が土地の斜面から出てくるが，ここでのみ，円弧の幾何学形態がぶっきらぼうに断ち切られ，大きな窓が穿たれる。アトリエの天井は，円弧を描く壁に沿ってトップライトのスリットが切れ，差し込む光が，剥き出しの抽象的な空間に複雑に交錯した曲面の図形を描く。

　大規模な「小篠邸」でも，安藤が極めて小規模な「住吉の長屋」で提示し展開させていた三つの建築的主題をもう一度見出すことはむずかしくない。自然光の調整。これは，他に例を見ない習熟を示し，暗示の効果すら生むに至っている。次に，中庭の形での「人工化された」自然の導入。これは，大阪の小さな長屋住宅で可能だったものよりさらに巧みに組み込み，一体化されている。そして最後に，構築された形態が示唆し，実際に住み手に強く影響を与える，新しいライフ・スタイルの探求。これは，数年前の住吉の場合と比較して，情け容赦なくという印象は弱くなったが，しかし同じ程度の決断をもって進められている。

　「小篠邸」はあの「住吉の長屋」の「洗練された不便さ」をより大規模に再現したにすぎないと主張することも，実際，不可能ではない。これは，そのウィットに富んだ響きから感じられるほどの誇張を含んでいない。まさにその通りだと思われる点が少なくない。たとえば，あの最初の主棟と従棟を結ぶ地下の暗い廊下は，住吉の長屋の中庭に似た，機能的に攪乱する障害物なのではないか。あるいはまた，南側の従棟を埋める八つの同一の極小で，スパルタ風に厳しい個室ユニットも，同じく「洗練された不便さ」を内包していないか。それらは，「住吉の長屋」の四角い箱だけの諸室と同じような慎重な調整によっても，たぶん夏の暑さから逃れられないと思うが，特に冬の寒さは大丈夫なのだろうか。そもそも，山の中の贅沢な週末住宅の大きな空間でも，大都市の中心部にある小規模住宅の極限まで抑えられた空間と同じ本質性，簡素さ，暗さという質を秘めているのではないか。これまで詳しく見たように，「小篠邸」のより大きな建築的可能性が，小さい（しかし，それだけに効果の上では劣らない）「住吉の長屋」に生命を吹き込んでいたのと同じ禁欲的な理想のために使われている。

〈城戸崎邸〉
「小篠邸」に関して述べてきた内容は，そのまま「城戸崎邸」にも当てはまる。これもまた，明らかに小さいとも貧しいとも言えないものである。東京の高級住宅街の一つである世田谷の610平方メートルの敷地に，延床面積が556平方メートルという住宅である。それでもなお，簡素さ，規律，禁欲主義について語ることができるのだろうか。

　安藤の特徴をもつこの3番目の住宅を，実際に訪問してみよう。まず静かな，

the outside. Although a later addition and not part of the original design, it seems to be a logical conclusion and organic extension of the house. It contains the workroom of the mistress of the house, a designer, and a small bathroom. The enclosed area is almost wholly buried and is therefore shut off by stark concrete walls. Only in the east where the slope exposes the architecture as a sand dune exposes archaeological remains, is the semicircular shape brusquely interrupted and the wall rent by a large window. Along the curved wall a narrow skylight allows a disturbing shaft of ever-changing light to filter into the bare and abstract space.

In this great structure of *the Koshino House* it is not difficult to find again the three architectural themes stated (and developed) by Ando in the minuscule *Row House in Sumiyoshi*: the modulation of natural light, here made to achieve effects of rare mastery and suggestion; the inclusion of "artificialized" nature into the architecture in the form of the inner courtyard, here much more skillfully incorporated than it was possible to do in the small row house in Osaka; and finally the search for a new lifestyle which the constructed form suggests and in fact imposes on the inhabitants, perhaps less implacably but certainly with no less determination than a few years previously at Sumiyoshi.

It can in fact be maintained that *the Koshino House* merely reproduces the refined inconvenience of *the Row House in Sumiyoshi* on a larger scale. This is less of an exaggeration than its witty tone might suggest. Is not the dark underground corridor which connects the two main parts of the building perhaps a functional obstacle similar to the inner courtyard of the row house? Are not too perhaps the eight identical minuscule and spartan rooms which occupy almost all the southern wing of the house? Are they not perhaps isolated from the heat of summer but above all from the cold of winter with the same deliberate moderation as the plain small rooms of *the Row House in Sumiyoshi*? Do not perhaps the large spaces of the opulent weekend house in the mountains also harbor the same qualities of essentiality, simplicity and starkness as the infinitely smaller spaces in the little house in the center of the great city? The greater architectural potential of *the Koshino House* has, when viewed closely, been pressed into service of the same ascetic ideal which inspired the more lowly (but thereby no less effective) *Row House in Sumiyoshi*.

Kidosaki House
The same comments apply to *the Kidosaki House* as to *the Koshino House*. This again can certainly not be said to be either small or poor. 556 square meters of useful surface on a 610-square-meter site at Setagaya, one of the most desirable residential areas in Tokyo. Is it still possible to talk again of simplicity, discipline and asceticism?

Let us visit this third house which bears Ando's stamp. We will have to enter a quiet and gently hilly part of the city where a rather close-set mesh of surprisingly narrow streets bounds regular groups of plots occupied almost exclusively by single family houses set in small, extremely well-tended gardens. The plot which is our

少し高くなった住宅街に入ると，通りは驚くほど狭く，それがかなり稠密な網の目を形づくっているが，敷地区画はかなり整然としており，ほとんどが戸建住宅で，それぞれが非常によく手入れされた小さな庭を伴っている。われわれの目指す住宅の敷地は，ほぼ正方形に近いが若干ゆがみがある。その敷地全体が，打放しコンクリートの壁によって囲い込まれ，内部空間を外部のあらゆる不躾な視線から守っている。その壁が一箇所で内側に湾曲していくが，ちょうど内部に招き入れる「じょうご」のような形になっている。それに吸い込まれるように入っていくと幅の広い階段があり，そこを下りたところが，1階に配された二つの住居の玄関前の内庭になる。この「じょうご」の湾曲する擁壁の内側には，上方に向かうもう一つの湾曲した狭い階段があり，これを上がると2階に置かれた住居の玄関に達する。

この住宅は，実際，三つの居住ユニットで構成されている。その一つは夫婦，もう一つは夫の父，そして妻の母の住居である。夫婦の住居はより大きく，2階に，その親たちの二つの住宅は1階に置かれる。ガレージ，地下室，オープン・スペースなどは共用である。

機能上のテーマは，家族全員が同じ屋根の下で生活しつつ，各々が必要なプライバシーを確保していることであった。安藤は，三つの完全に独立した住居を空間的に融合することで，それを達成している。父の住居は，居間，食堂，寝室，浴室，キッチンから構成され，すべて1階に置かれている。外に対しては，道路側の光庭と敷地の南側にあって注意深く樹木が植えられた広い中庭に面している。母の住居は，部屋の構成は父の家と同じだが2層吹抜けた居間を中心に構成されており，この居間も大きな開口を通して南側の広い中庭に面する。夫

婦の住居は，父，母の住居とほぼ同じだが，互いに分離した居間と食堂，そして書斎の存在などが異なり，全体として2階と3階にまたがって配されている。2階で住居はテラスに面しているが，たとえば食堂のオープン・スペースが東の方向に伸び広がる可能性を示唆する。3階でも，住居はもう一つの大きなテラスに面する。この場合，テラスはコンクリート壁に囲まれ，完全なプライバシーを確保するためのものである。居間の壁は大きく湾曲し（この壁は，玄関まで沿って歩いた，あの壁である），この湾曲する壁に沿ってトップライトのスリットが切り込まれ，差し込む陽光が，くっきりと明暗をつくっている。さらに，居間は吹抜けの小さな光庭に面しているが，光庭は，下にある父の寝室に自然光を与えるものである。

このように複雑な機能プログラムを解くために，安藤は，人の心を解放し安らかにする「簡素さ」を備えた形態プランをデザインしている。一辺12メートルの立方体が，敷地の形状に沿って領域を囲い取る壁との間に，生活を保護するために注意深く調整された空間が生まれるような形で，敷地の中心に置かれている。立方体は，いつものように，内も外もすべて，打放しの鉄筋コンクリートでつくられている（唯一の例外は母の住居で，ここでは粗い灰色が老婦人を当惑させないように，白色プラスターでインテリアが仕上げられている）。サッシュ関係は，暗い灰色の塗装が施されている。床は，暗色の薄いスレート（玄昌石）か木（ナラ）のフローリングで優美に仕上げられ，しかも，地盤として支えるコンクリートから遊離しない水平面を形成している。落ち着いた木製の収納壁も同じく建築家のデザインによる。

人を安らかにする簡素な建物，そう言ってよいだろう。しかし，この簡素さ（単純さ）は，部屋がもう一つの部屋の中に，中庭がもう一つの中庭の中に，そして住居がもう一つの住居の中に，という実に精妙な空間配置を内に含んでいる。自

goal is a slightly irregular square completely enclosed by a bare reinforced concrete wall which protects the interior from any indiscreet gaze. The wall only curves inward at one point, inviting access to a kind of funnel which gives way to a wide staircase leading to an inner garden onto which the entrances to the two apartments located on the ground floor open. Immediately alongside the curvature of the wall there is also a kind of narrow passage divided from the access funnel by a solid breast wall, also of concrete. Scaling the steps of a second stairway, which is parallel to the first but offset with respect to it, this passage leads to the apartment located on the first floor.

This is in fact a house consisting of three residential units: one for a couple, another for his father and yet another for her mother. The couple occupy the larger apartment, the one on the first floor. The two elders occupy the two apartments on the ground floor. The garage, the basement and the open spaces are used in common.

The functional theme consisted of bringing all the members of the family to live under the same roof, but offering each the necessary privacy. Ando has achieved this by spatially fusing together three independent apartments. The father's apartment, which consists of a living and dining room, bedroom, bath and kitchen, is all on the ground floor and opens onto both a small light well made on the street side and an extensive carefully planted courtyard on the southern side of the site. The mother's apartment, which has the same elements as the father's apartment, is organized around a space of double height which also faces the southern courtyard

through a large window. This space provides direct communication to the couple's apartment in its upper level. The couple's apartment, which also has a dining area separate from the living room, and a study, in addition to the rooms in the other apartments, extends over two levels on the first and second floor. On the first floor it faces a terrace which suggests a sort of extension of the open space of the dining area to the east. On the second floor it faces another very large terrace which is completely enclosed by concrete walls and therefore absolutely private. The living room, which is bounded by a curved wall (the one which forms the entrance), onto which a skylight throws a glancing shaft of light, opens onto the same small courtyard which illuminates the bedroom in the father's flat.

To achieve such a complex functional program Ando has designed a formal plan of disarming simplicity——a twelve by twelve meter cube placed almost exactly in the center of the plot in such a way as to create a sequence of carefully modulated protective spaces around it. The cube is, as usual, all constructed of bare reinforced concrete, both externally and internally (the only exception being the mother's apartment, which is surfaced with white plaster). The frames are of metal painted dark gray. The flooring is of dark slate or elegant wood laid in such a way as to allow immediate access to the underlying surfaces. Even the sober wooden wall cupboards have been designed by the architect.

A building, one might say, of disarming simplicity, but this simplicity incorporates an extremely sophisticated positioning of a room within another, a courtyard within another, an apartment

らの明快な幾何学をいかすために，その平面と断面に現れているように，安藤は，ピラネージ的特徴を帯びるに至った「空間機械」を考案する必要があった。すべてのサービスを床下とか打放しコンクリート壁の背後に隠す必要，またそこから生じた見えない空間，ダクト，二重天井を用意する必要などによって，ピラネージ的な特性はさらに高められた。そのすべてが鉄筋コンクリートでつくられ，それ故に，現場での安易な修正は許されない。「城戸崎邸」の設計は（安藤はいつも工事をするのに必要なすべての原図をホルダーに入れて保管しているが，この作品のすばらしい原図がその一つに含まれている），1982年から1985年まで，たっぷり4年間を要している。

簡素さ（単純さ），実際それは大変な努力によって生み出されたものだ。薄れることのない，強烈に望んで生まれた簡素さ，そのような簡素さが，この裕福な住宅でさえも，むしろその豊かさを見せびらかさないために人工的に創造し，注意深く表現されている。

その豊かさが住み手を圧倒し困惑させないこと。ここで再び，すでに住吉と芦屋で試みたように，安藤は自らの建築を慎み深く質素な生活に合わせている。温かく柔らかい仕上げの壁はなく，ブラインド，シャッター，カーテンの付いた窓もなく，空間効果を混乱させたり，でしゃばる仕上げはない。中庭にせよテラスにせよ，いずれも内向的な世界であって，それ自体で完結している。周辺の地形が傾斜しているために町の大部分を見渡せるはずの上の広いテラスからも，何も見えない。全体が灰色の打放しコンクリート壁に取り囲まれて，視線を妨げられているからだ。唯一可能なのは，それも苦労してのことだが，東と西の壁に開けた三つの不可解なスリットを通して景色を眺めることである。同じことが，構

成原理と力学の法則に逆らってまで南の中庭を囲む周壁の隅部に開けられた狭いスリットについても言える。それは，その壁が本体ではなく翼部でしかないことを強調するかのようだが，そのスリットから通りの風景を眺めることが期待されているとは思えない。禁欲主義者は町の眺めを楽しまない。ル・コルビュジエがシャルル・ド・ブイステギ氏に認めた，あの潜望鏡による選び切り取られた眺めの楽しみすら禁じられている。その代わりに彼は，形而上学的なコンクリート枠の中で，次々に変化して見せる空を観察する。その方が得るものが大きいだろうが。

〈職能：芸術家〉
16世紀に，日本の関西地方（安藤の生地，大阪を含む地方）で，当時の偉大な権力者であった豊臣秀吉と茶の宗匠として彼の庇護を受ける千利休が，侘（わび）の理念を確立し，それを精力的に広め，まもなく多くの弟子を輩出するに至った。この侘は，簡素，貧困，謙虚を最高の美徳としたが，それは，富を見せびらかす低俗さの対極に立つものである。それはまた，制度化した権力への不満と独裁者への抵抗という意味も含んでいる。商人と政治家の無感動な世界から拒否され苦しめられていた芸術家＝知識人は，侘の境界内で，自らを切り離したいと切望するものに公然と挑戦しつつ独自の宇宙を築き上げた。その宇宙では，自己鍛錬と厳格さが，精神的（倫理的）強さと苦行的（禁欲的）な洗練になっている。

その生まれと性格から，安藤忠雄は，なお生きているこの伝統に属する。日本的伝統を生かそうとするファッション界のニューリーダーたちも同じで，彼らは安藤のクライアントでもある。ヒロコ・コシノもその一人である。彼が自ら建築に，現存する最も貧しく，平凡なコンクリートという材料を選んでいるのも偶然で

within another. To take advantage of the clear geometry of his design, Ando has had to invent a spatial machinery which, as revealed by the plans and section, proves to have Piranesian characteristics. These are heightened by the necessity of concealing all the services beneath the floors and behind the bare walls, and therefore the need to create invisible spaces, ducts and double ceilings. All of this, by the way, in reinforced concrete, and therefore without any possibility of correction on site. It is not surprising that the design of *the Kidosaki House* (splendidly documented in one of the folders in which Ando is accustomed to gather all the drawings required for the construction of a building) took all of four years, from 1982 to 1985.

A simplicity, in fact, which is achieved with great effort. An unflagging, strongly desired simplicity. A simplicity, even in this other wealthy house, artificially created and deliberately displayed so as not to show off its wealth.

And also not to cause that wealth to overwhelm its inhabitants. Here again, as already at Sumiyoshi and Ashiya, Ando constrains his architecture to an abstemious life. No softly finished walls, no windows "clothed" with blinds, shutters and curtains, no disturbing or intrusive fittings. There is even nothing to be seen outside. The courtyards and the terraces are introverted worlds, complete in themselves, and neither can anything be seen from the large upper terrace which could overlook a large part of the city because of the slight incline between them. This is prevented by high solid walls, cast in bare gray concrete. It is only possible, and with difficulty, to

squint at the view through the three enigmatic slots with which Ando pierces the two eastern and western walls, in the same way as one can look onto the street through the narrow gaps left against all the rules of construction and laws of statics at the corners of the perimeter wall enclosing the southern courtyard, as if to emphasize its relegation to the wings. The ascetic does not enjoy a view of the city, even the selected view through the periscope which Le Corbusier allowed Charles de Buistegui; instead he observes, with greater profit, an ever-changing sky set in its metaphysical concrete frame.

Profession: Artist
In the sixteenth century in the Japanese province of Kansai (which includes Osaka, Ando's birthplace), the great warlord Toyotomi Hideyoshi and his protégé, the tea master Sen no Rikyu, created the discipline of *wabi* and promoted it vigorously, soon to be followed by numerous disciples. The term implies adherence to the virtues of simplicity, poverty, and modesty which are opposed to the vulgar ostentation of wealth. It also has the connotation of dissatisfaction with institutional power, and resistance to tyranny. Within the bounds of *wabi* the artist-intellectual, rejected and vexed by the unresponsive world of merchants and politicians, can create his own universe, openly challenging that from which he longs to dissociate himself, where self-discipline and rigor become moral strength and ascetic refinement.

Through his birth and inclination Tadao Ando belongs to this

はない．また，その材料で，最も単純で要素的な形態をつくっていることも，偶然ではない．さらに，彼がそれを，装飾も被覆も施さずに裸のままでオープンにしているのも，同じく偶然ではないのである．と同時に，しかしながら彼は，芸術家としての自分の役割を強く主張している．彼の設計する住宅は，それを構成する材料ではなく，その材料に形態を与える理念の故に，価値があるのである．その禁欲的な特性は，付随的なものではなくて，本質であり，内容そのものである．そのデザインの背後には，この詩人の専門家気質があるに違いない．

これが，見掛けの上品さではなく，ピントのずれた美化でもなく，安藤が自らの本質と感じているものである．つまり，全くの一個人であり，一つの伝統の申し子である．自らが深く根を下ろしていると感じながらも，その建築的遺構をコピーしたのでは再生できないことを知っている伝統．いずれにしても，安藤にとっては，過去を模倣する問題は決して起こり得ない．自分が伝統の強力な連鎖を構成する一つの輪であることを知っている彼のような人間は，自らへの社会的信頼を高めるために，過去の文化の断片を現在にこれ見よがしに移してみせる必要はない．彼自身が行うものは，必然的に侘である．彼がなすべきことは，自らの建築家，より正確には建築家＝芸術家としての適性を，その能力の限界まで発揮することである．さらに何が必要だろうか．簡素，貧困，厳格という侘の理想は，まさに時間を超越した理想であって，近代建築運動と同様に古代エジプトの建築にも適用可能なものだ．ピュリスムは一つのスタイルではなくて一つの姿勢である．それは歴史的モーメントではなくて詩的本質に属している．それに自らを捧げる者ならば，過去と現在あるいは伝統と革新の間で選択などはしないものだ．彼は，弁証法を超越し，弁証法の用語を無意味化してしまう．

しかしながら，侘の理想は，東洋と同様に西洋においても有効であって，多くの文化にアピールし得る理想である．この理想に従うことは，自らの文化に固執するかそれとも異なる外国の文化に門戸を開くかという選択を避けることでもあるのだ．つまりそれは，自らのアイデンティティと心を失わずに，押さえがたく湧き起こる好奇心に身を委ねる，いわばそのような贅沢を自他に許容しうることを意味している．事実，安藤は異なる領域とか異なる文化の間を注意深く確実に，魚のように泳ぎ回っているように思われる．彼はそこで出会う何事にも関心を示しながら，決して過剰な熱情に屈することはない．自らの内部に有する簡素さの理想を静かに，しかし飽くことなく追い続けながら，彼は，メソポタミアからギリシャまでの古代文明の建築，16世紀日本からイタリア・ルネサンス，マルク＝アントワーヌ・ロジエの素朴な田舎屋からクロード＝ニコラ・ルドゥとかエチエンヌ＝ルイ・ブレーらのユートピア，アドルフ・ロースからルイス・カーンに至る厳格さ，そのあらゆるものから自らが競い凌駕すべき対象を見出している．このような参照の対象の多様性は彼を進むべき道から逸らせるのではなく，むしろそれを確かなものにしている．そしてまた，彼に知的な強さを与えているのである．

『オメロ・バルケッタ』という物語の中で，アルベルト・サヴィーニオは，その主人公に精神が満ち足りて生きることのできる場所の必要性について自伝的に内省させている．「われわれは，なんと愚かしく漫然と生きていることか」とメーロは考える．「もし寒ければ，われわれは暖められた場所に避難し，寒さが我が身に及ばぬようにする．もし暑ければ，同じように，われわれは涼しい場所に避難する．しかし，その時の適度な暖かさも涼しさも，決してわれわれの精神までは保護しないし，それを脅威あるいは破壊から守ることもない．われわれの精

---

still living tradition, as do many of the protagonists of the new Japanese fashion who are his clients, above all Hiroko Koshino. It is not by chance that he has chosen the poorest and most commonplace material in existence, concrete, for his architecture. It is not by chance that he fashions this into the most simple and elementary shapes. It is not by chance that he leaves it bare, open, devoid of all decoration or covering. At the same time however Ando lays vigorous claim to his own role as an artist. His houses are of value not because of the materials of which they are made, but because of the ideas to which they give material form. Their ascetic qualities are not something extra, they are their essence and their very substance. Behind their design must lie the professionalism of the poet.

This is what Ando, without false modesty and even without pointless glorification, feels himself to be——a single individual and the offspring of a tradition. A tradition which knows that it cannot find revival by copying the architectural remains in which it feels its own roots nevertheless to be profoundly fixed. In any case, for Ando the question of imitating the past never arises. Someone like himself who knows he is a link in the chain of tradition has no need to literally transport fragments into the present in order to bolster his own credibility. What he himself does is, inevitably, *wabi*. All he has to do is to pursue his vocation as an architect, or more specifically as an architect-artist, to the best of his ability. What more is needed? The *wabi* ideals of simplicity, poverty and rigor are exquisitely timeless ideals which can be applied to the architecture of ancient Egypt as equally to Modernism. Purism is not a style, it is an attitude. It

does not refer to an historical moment, but to poetry. Anyone who devotes himself to it does not choose between the past and the present, between tradition and invention, he transcends dialectic, making its terms meaningless.

But the ideals of *wabi* are also ideals which appeal to many cultures, being as valid in the West as in the East. To follow them also avoids the alternatives of clinging to one's own culture or opening the door to different and foreign cultures. It means instead being able to grant oneself the luxury of indulging extensive curiosity without thereby losing one's own identity and heart. Truly Ando seems to move like a fish between different eras and different cultures, attentive and secure, allowing himself to be tempted by everything which he meets along his way and yet not yielding to any temptation. By quietly and indefatigably following the ideal of simplicity which he bears within himself, he finds examples to emulate everywhere: from the architecture of the ancient civilizations from Mesopotamia to Greece, from sixteenth-century Japan to the Italian Renaissance, from the rustic cabin of Marc-Antoine Laugier to the utopia of Claude-Nicolas Ledoux and Etienne-Louis Boullée, from the rigor of Adolf Loos to Louis Kahn. This multiplicity of references does not distract him from his path, they confirm him on it. And they also give him more intellectual strength to follow it.

In the tale "Omero Barchetta," Alberto Savinio makes his hero autobiographically reflect on the need for places where the mind can live content. "How foolishly and heedlessly we live!" thinks Mero, "If it is cold we take refuge in a heated place and ensure that

神的安寧は，過ぎゆく暗い影，響き渡る騒音，そして開け放たれたドアのなすがままになっている。……身体的な快適さに対しては，家，家具，暖冷房の手段，人工照明がある。しかし，精神的幸福を保護し確かなものにするために，人間は何を発明し生産してきたか」。安藤忠雄は，サヴィーニオのこの思慮深い主人公の熱心な忠告をしっかりと心に受け止めているように見える。その建築全般，とくに「住吉の長屋」「小篠邸」「城戸崎邸」において，安藤は精神の充足を求め，身体的な快適さを注意深く避けている。さらに言えば，彼は精神に喜びを与えるために，身体に喜びを与える手立てを，細心の注意を払って，できるだけ少なくしようとしている。

　根っからの小市民であり消費主義の典型と同時に奴隷となった，20世紀の標準的人間は，こう言っても鼻であしらうだろう。だが，それはどうでもよい。安藤の住宅は，彼らのために建てられたのではない。半世紀前のル・コルビュジエとかミース・ファン・デル・ローエの場合と同様，それは，新しい理想の人間のために建てられたものだ。すぐに退屈なものに変わり省みられなくなる見栄だけの空虚なものを一杯集めるよりも，二，三の完全な形態と少量の優れた物を好む人間。様式の連続性を信じ流行のきまぐれな変化を意に介さない人間。生産と利用の法則に結びつかない表面的な発明ではなく，十分に確立された技術を使った優れた出来栄えの仕事を，適切に評価する人間。外観よりも本質を信じる人間。身体以上に魂を大切にする人間。実際，なかなか見出すのがむずかしい人間。しかし，にもかかわらず，恐ろしい戦争に常に揺り動かされ，生態的な大破滅の予感に脅えるわれわれの世界がますます必要とする人間。彼にこそ，われわれは，可能であり受け入れ得る未来の希望を託すべきだろう。

安藤忠雄の建築は全般的に，そして「住吉の長屋」『小篠邸』『城戸崎邸』はとくに，この理想の人間のいわば最初の具体化をめざして設計し建設されたものであって，来るべき未来を構築する視覚化された要素と考えてよかろう。それらは，もの静かに，希望の建築となっているのである。

和訳：川向正人

註：
本文中の引用は以下の文献より行なった。
Karl Kraus, *Der Untergang des Abendlands*
Tadao Ando, 'Light and Wind'；セルジュ・サラとフランソワーズ・ラベによる，1988年1月25日から3月20日までボルドーのアントルポ・レネで開催された，安藤忠雄展のカタログ（Arc en Rêve publications）に収録，p.38
Tadao Ando, 'The Emotionally Made Architectural Spaces of Tadao Ando,' *The Japan Architect*, April 1980, pp.45-46
Alberto Savinio, 'Omero Barchetta,' in: *Casa La Vita*, Edizioni Adelphi, Milan 1988, pp.209-210

the cold does not reach us. We do the same if it is hot, taking refuge in a cool place. But propitious warmth and coolness does not in any way protect our mind, or preserve it from threats and destruction. Our mental well-being is at the mercy of a passing shadow, a resounding noise, an opening door,...for bodily comfort there are houses, furniture, means of heating and means of cooling, artificial light; but what has man invented, what has he manufactured, to safeguard and defend his mental happiness?" Tadao Ando appears to have taken the exhortation of Savinio's thoughtful hero to heart. In his architecture in general and specifically in *the House in Sumiyoshi*, *Koshino* and *Kidosaki Houses*, he has deliberately neglected bodily comfort in favor of spiritual comfort. More specifically, he has deliberately diminished the devices which give pleasure to the body in order to give pleasure to the mind.

The dyed-in-the-wool petit bourgeois, the tenacious exponent and slave of consumerism, the standard man of the twentieth century, will turn up his nose. This does not matter. Ando's houses are not built for him. Like the houses of Le Corbusier or Mies van der Rohe more than half a century before him, they are built for a new, ideal man. One who prefers a few perfect forms and a small number of outstanding objects to the amassing of pretentious and inane things which soon become boring and are discarded. A man who believes in the continuity of style and ignores the vagaries of fashion. A man who appreciates work well done using well-established techniques, and not superficial invention without connection with the rules of production and use. A man who believes in essentials rather than appearances. A man who takes better care of his soul than his body. A man, in fact, who is still rarely to be found. But nevertheless a man which our world endlessly shaken by dreadful wars and insidiously threatened by an ecological apocalypse increasingly needs, and on whom we should found our hopes for a future which is both possible and acceptable.

The architecture of Tadao Ando in general and *the House in Sumiyoshi*, *Koshino* and *Kidosaki Houses* in particular, designed and constructed to host some first embodiment of this ideal man, are to be included among those physical elements of which some kind of future might conceivably be built. They have thus silently become the architecture of hope.

Quotations in the text are drawn from the following:
Karl Kraus, *Der Untergang des Abendlands*
Tadao Ando, 'Light and Wind,' in *Ando par/by Ando*, catalog of the "Tadao Ando" exhibition at the Entrepôt Lainé in Bordeaux from 25 January to 20 March 1988, by Serge Salat and Françoise Labbé, Arc en Rêve publications, p. 38
Tadao Ando, 'The Emotionally Made Architectural Spaces of Tadao Ando,' *The Japan Architect*, April 1980, pp. 45-46
Alberto Savinio, 'Omero Barchetta,' in *Casa La Vita*, Edizioni Adelphi, Milan 1988, pp. 209-210

Row House in Sumiyoshi
1975-76

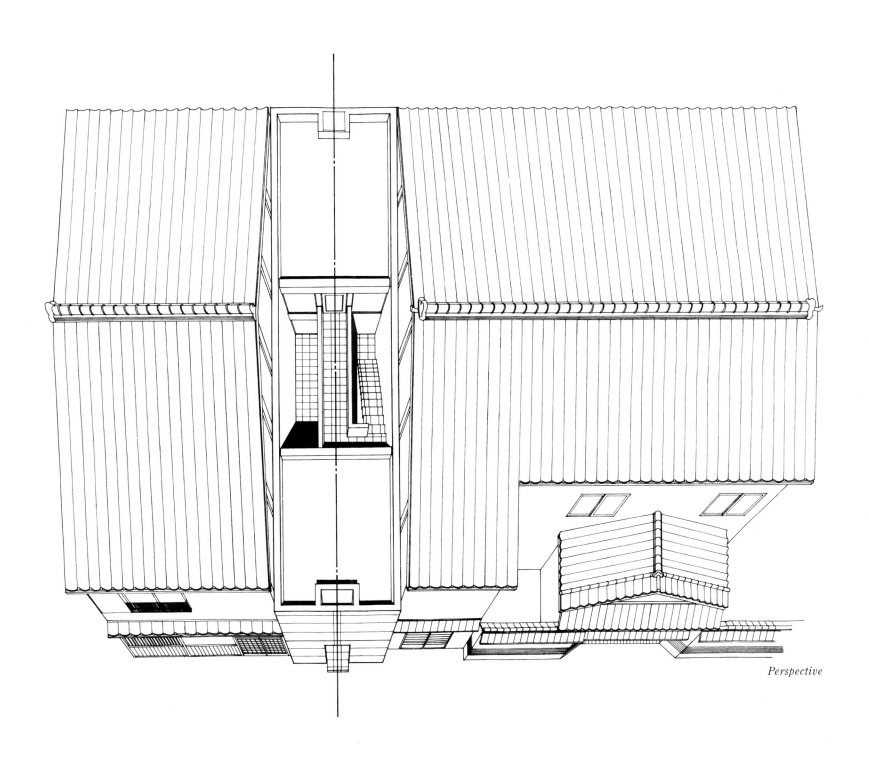

Perspective

Street view, late 1970s

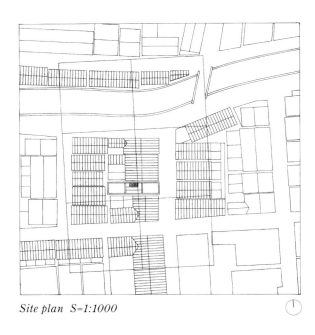

Site plan S=1:1000

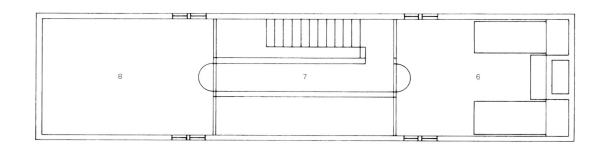

Second floor

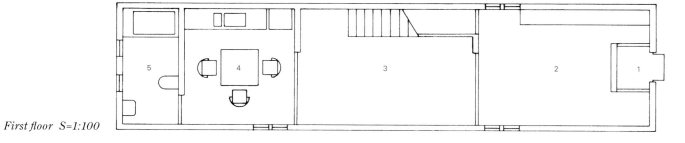

First floor S=1:100

1 ENTRANCE
2 LIVING ROOM
3 COURT
4 KITCHEN/DINING ROOM
5 BATHROOM
6 MASTER BEDROOM
7 BRIDGE
8 BEDROOM

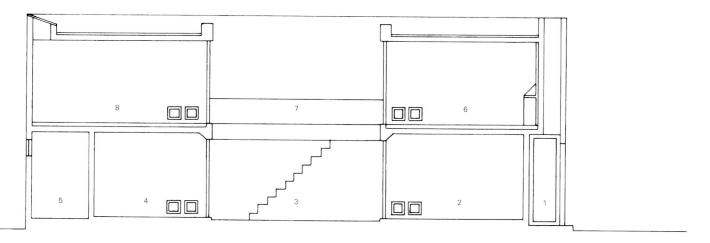

Section S=1:100

Front elevation, late 1970s

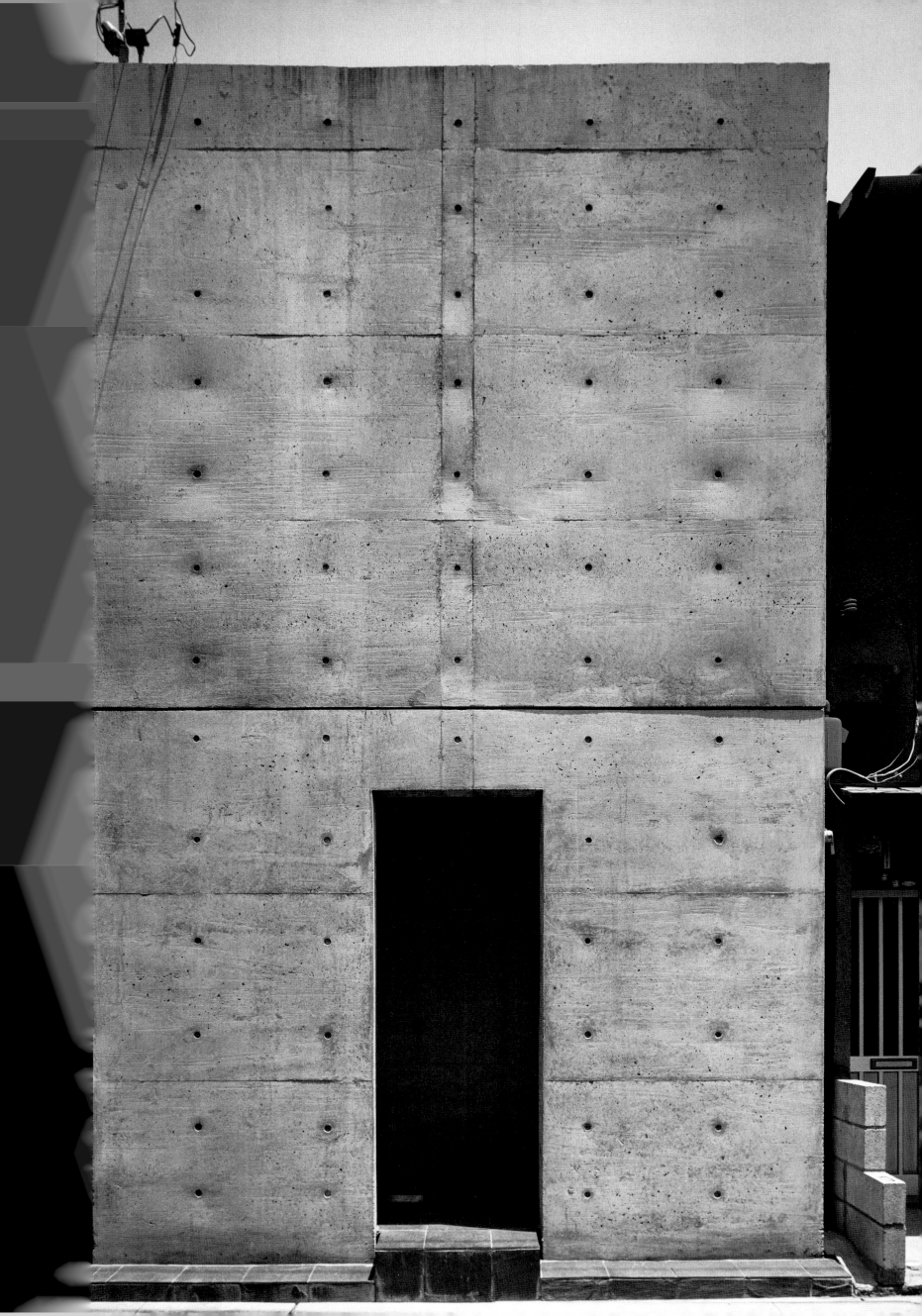

Living room. Looking kitchen/dining room through court, late 1970s

Dining room, late 1970s

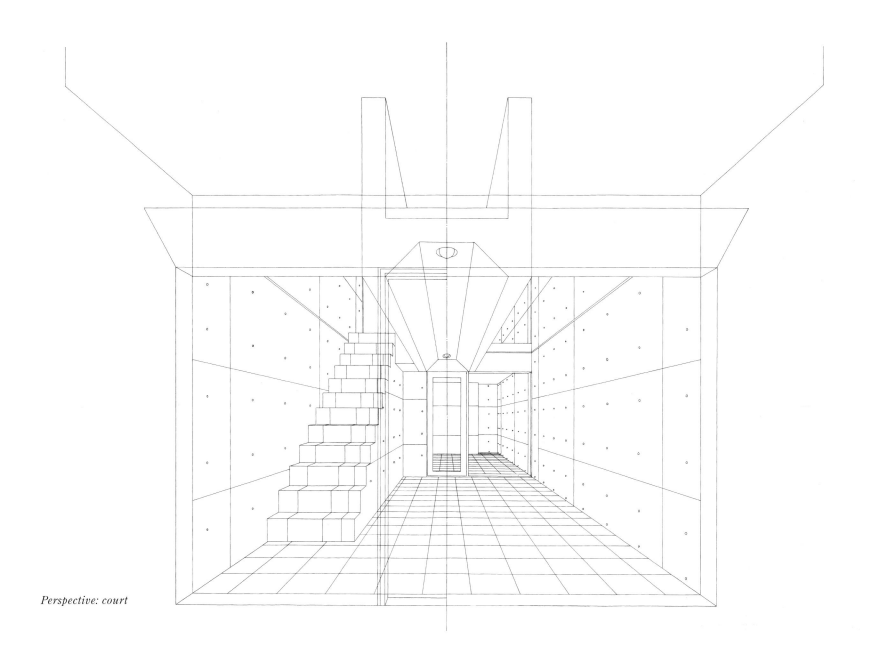

Perspective: court

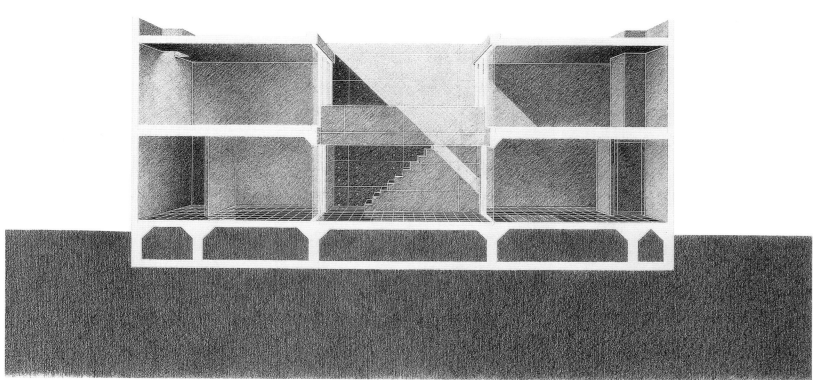

Sectional perspective S=1:100

Second floor. Bridge between bedrooms, late 1970s

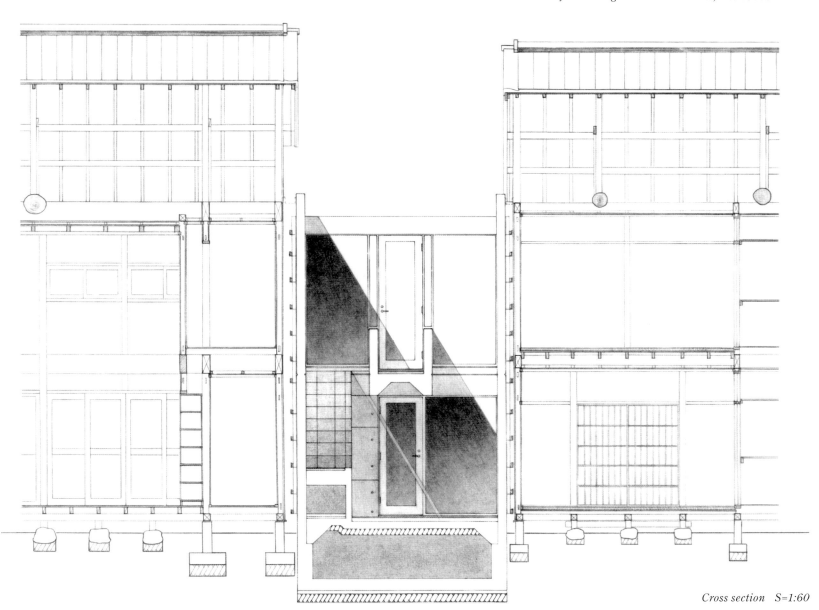

Cross section   S=1:60

Court, 1993

Void above court. Looking master bedroom, late 1970s

Koshino House
1979-81/1983-84/2004-06

Overall view from west, 1985

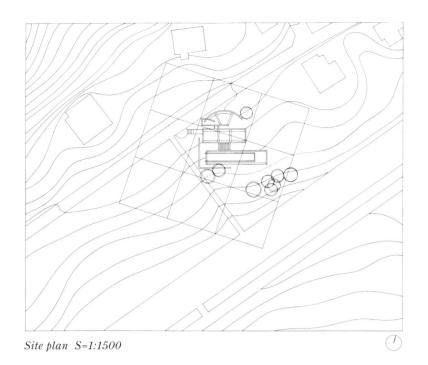

Site plan S=1:1500

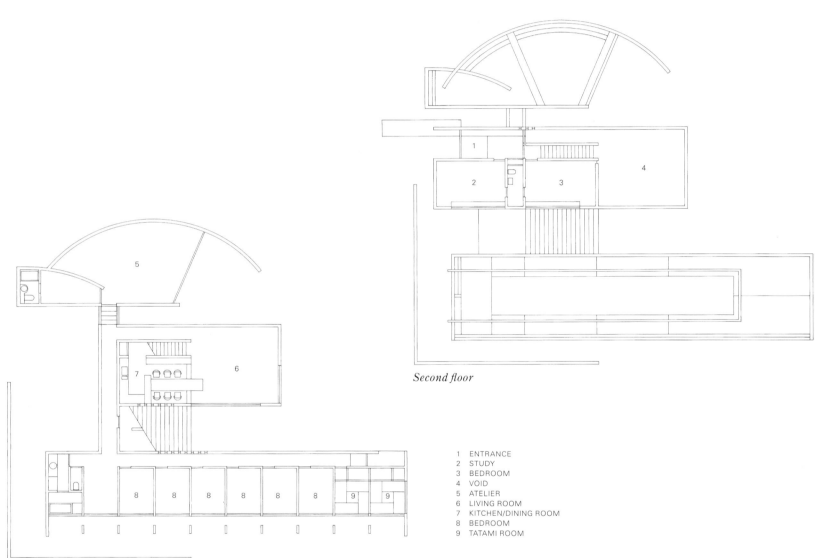

Second floor

1 ENTRANCE
2 STUDY
3 BEDROOM
4 VOID
5 ATELIER
6 LIVING ROOM
7 KITCHEN/DINING ROOM
8 BEDROOM
9 TATAMI ROOM

First floor S=1:250

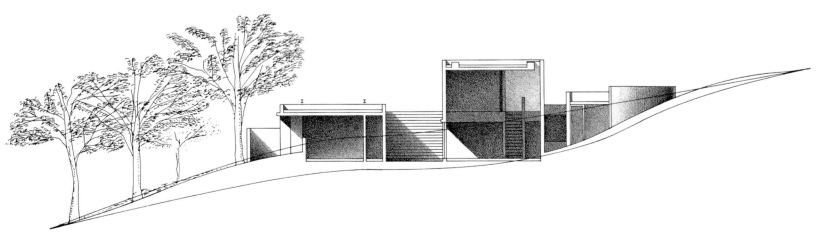

Section S=1:200

Aerial view, 1985

Stairs between bedroom wing (above) and living room wing, 1983

Stairs and court. Bedroom wing on right, living room wing on left, 1993

Night view from garden on east, 1993

Entrance, 1993

Entrance, 1983

Void above living room. Looking from staircase, 1993

Living room, 1993

Living room with skylight, 1983

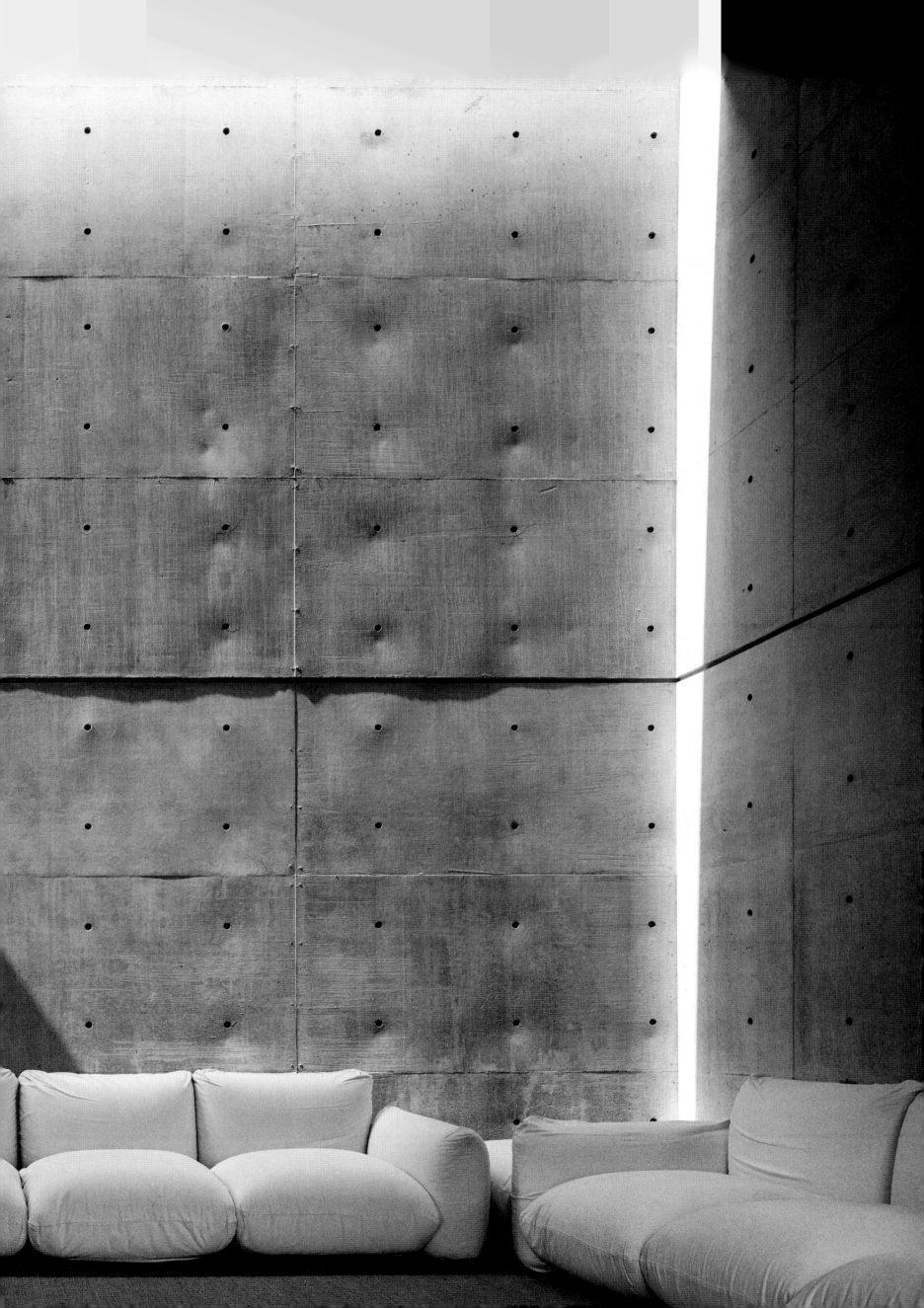

Living room. View toward dining room, 1993

Dining room, 1983

Staircase to entrance. Dining room on left, hallway on right leads to atelier, 1993

Atelier, 1985

Guest house entrance, 2006

Hall of guest house, 2006

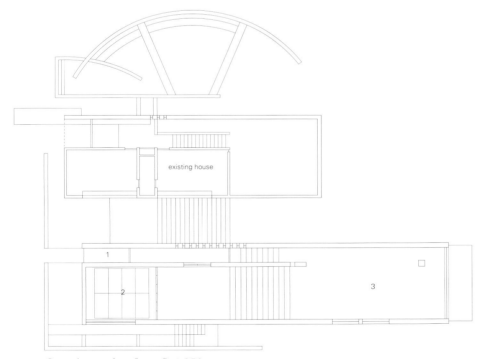

Guest house: first floor S=1:250

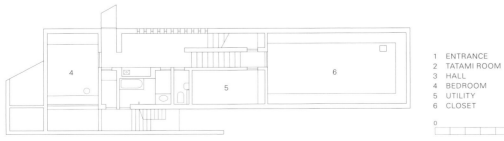

Guest house: basement

1 ENTRANCE
2 TATAMI ROOM
3 HALL
4 BEDROOM
5 UTILITY
6 CLOSET

Hall of guest house, 2006

View from garden on east, 2006.
Guest house (left) was newly built at same height as main building (right) when it was remodeled in 2004-06

Kidosaki House
1982-86

Street view, 1993

Street elevation, 1987

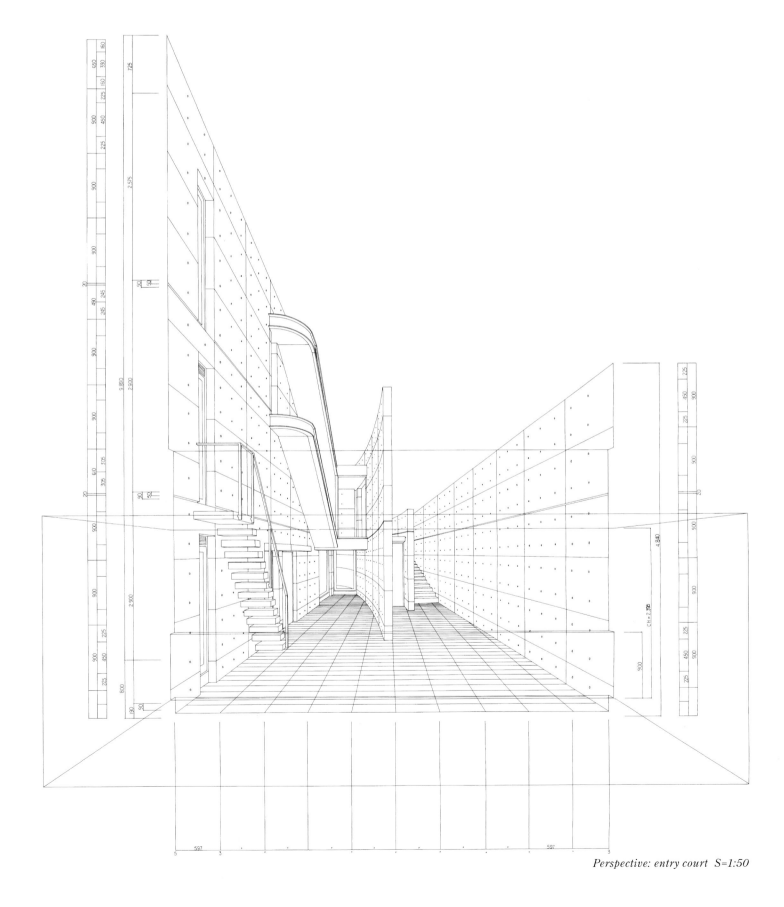

Perspective: entry court S=1:50

Entry court, 1987

Night view of entry court, 1987

Living room on first floor, 1993

Downward view of living room on first floor, 1993

Wall of living room with natural light from slits, 1987

Night view of living room, 1993

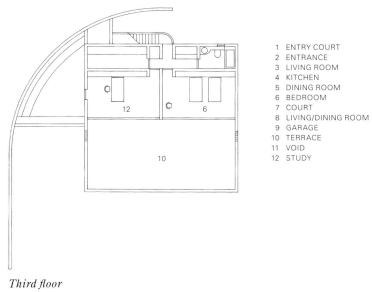

Third floor

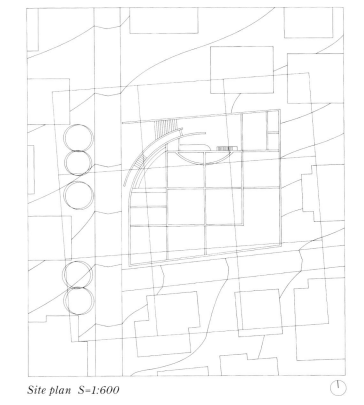

Site plan S=1:600

1 ENTRY COURT
2 ENTRANCE
3 LIVING ROOM
4 KITCHEN
5 DINING ROOM
6 BEDROOM
7 COURT
8 LIVING/DINING ROOM
9 GARAGE
10 TERRACE
11 VOID
12 STUDY

Second floor

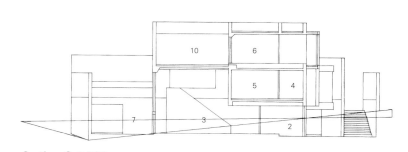

Section S=1:300

Section

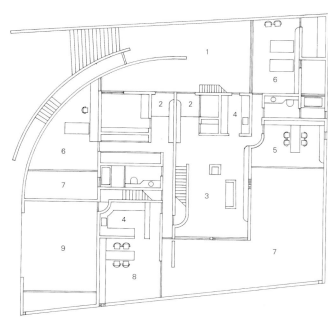

First floor S=1:300

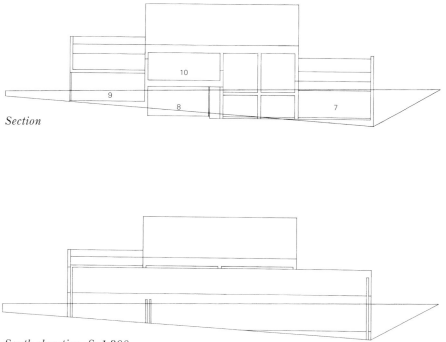

South elevation S=1:300

Court of dining room, 1987

Living room on second floor, 1993

Dining room on second floor, 1993

Dining room on second floor. View toward living room, 1987

Staircase to third floor, 1993

Terrace on third floor, 1987

Study on third floor, 1993

View toward study (left) and bedroom (right) from terrace on third floor, 1993

Photographs are taken by Yukio Futagawa except as noted below.
Cover, p.18, p.21, pp.22-23, p.25, pp.28-31, p.33, p.34, p.38 right, pp.42-43, p.46, pp.48-55, p.58, pp.60-61, p.66, p.71, p.75, p.77 above: photos by Yoshio Takase/GA photographers

'Three Houses by Tadao Ando' by Vittorio Magnago Lampugnani is reprinted from "GA 71 Tadao Ando Azuma House/Koshino House/Kidosaki House" (A.D.A. EDITA Tokyo, 1994)

ヴィットリオ・マニャーゴ・ランプニャーニによるエッセイ「安藤忠雄の三つの住宅」は，『GA 71 安藤忠雄 東邸（住吉の長屋）/小篠邸 / 城戸崎邸』（エーディーエー・エディタ・トーキョー発行，1994年）より再録

世界現代住宅全集 31
安藤忠雄
住吉の長屋
小篠邸
城戸崎邸
2021 年 3 月 25 日発行
文：ヴィットリオ・マニャーゴ・ランプニャーニ
撮影：二川幸夫
編集：二川由夫
アート・ディレクション：細谷巌

印刷・製本：大日本印刷株式会社
制作・発行：エーディーエー・エディタ・トーキョー
151-0051　東京都渋谷区千駄ヶ谷 3-12-14
TEL.（03）3403-1581（代）

ISBN 978-4-87140-564-5 C1352